SKYVILLE

1

THIS BOOK BELONGS TO:

_____

MAXWELL

The Firehouse Mouse

First Edition Printing, 2014

ISBN 978-0-9903374-0-9 (paperback)
ISBN-10: 0-9903374-0-5
Library of Congress Control Number: 2014913127

Inquiries may be addressed to:
Immaginare Works LLC
5510 NE Antioch Rd #216
Kansas City, MO 64119
www.ImmaginareWorksLLC.com

Dedication

For my wife, Grace, and my daughters, Laurena and Isabella.
Thank you for all of the never ending love
and support you give to me.-MSC

Deep in the vast, open country, over the green rolling meadows
stood a large farm.
Sure, this farm had the usual chickens and sheep, cows and horses,
orchards and vegetable fields.
However, this farm was different. It was run by
a family of hard working mice.

In this family were loving parents, Leo and Daisy,
and their three children,
Rudy, Lola and, the youngest, Maxwell.

Life on the farm was very hard, but it was rewarding.

Everyone had important chores to do.

Both big and strong,

Leo and Rudy were responsible for the plowing and planting.

Daisy and Lola were fast and efficient,
tending to the plants and quickly harvesting them when they were ready.

Now, you see, Maxwell was small and slimmer than the average mouse. Unfortunately, he was unable to perform most of the hard chores that farm life required.

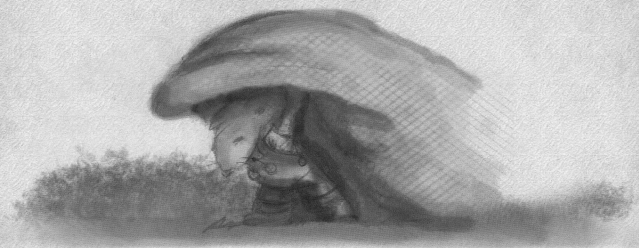

He wasn't strong enough to lift the bags of seed and sure wasn't tall enough to drive the tractor.

Leo would give Maxwell the easier tasks so that he could feel like he was a good helper. But Maxwell was smart, and he knew better.

"I just want to be somebody.
I just want to help," he would always say to himself.

One day, Maxwell decided the farm wasn't the place for him.

He always dreamed of living in a place where he would feel important. He often thought about living in the city. "There are people of all sizes and shapes that live there and so many places to work," he thought.

Maxwell was worried about how his mother and father would feel if he left the farm.

After talking about it with Leo and Daisy, Maxwell thankfully
received their blessing to move to
a nearby city called Skyville.
He packed up some of his belongings and left the
family farm to find his place in the city.

While walking on the side of a dirt road, he was greeted by Farmer Franklin who was on his way to Skyville to visit with family.

"Hop on in! I'll give you a ride!" he yelled in a loud, cheerful voice. Maxwell jumped and jumped but, because of his size, couldn't reach the floor of the truck. His head drooped down, and he said in a sad voice, "I'm too small. I can't jump that high."

All of a sudden, an outstretched hand neared Maxwell's small body.
It was the hand of Mrs. Franklin, who was also in the truck.

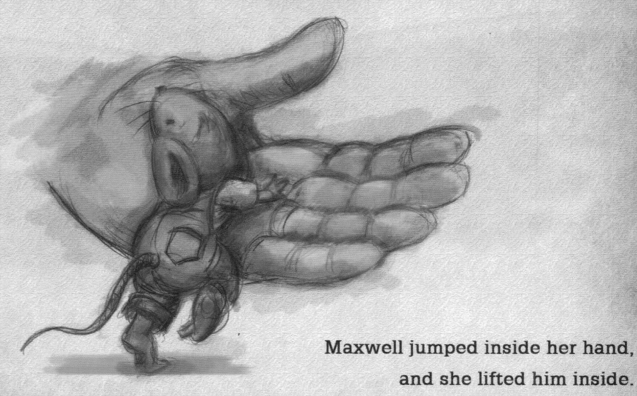

Maxwell jumped inside her hand,
and she lifted him inside.
Off they went; Maxwell's journey had begun.

Farmer Franklin dropped Maxwell off safely at a corner in the
middle of the city. He looked around in amazement.
There were so many people all around him.
The buildings were so tall they seemed to reach the clouds.

He had seen many twinkling stars light the night on the farm
but never this many lights during the daytime.
Food stands were all over the place.
He closed his eyes so that he could smell the delicious food in the air.
He sure was hungry from the long trip.

Maxwell opened his eyes.
All of a sudden he saw the bottom
of someone's shoe closely
approaching over the top of him!

He scurried to a nearby wall
to avoid being stepped on by
the people hustling around him.
"Boy that was close!"
he said huffing and puffing.

The size of the city began to scare him.

"Where do I go now?" he thought.

"Maybe it was a mistake coming to Skyville."

Maxwell took in a deep breath and decided to walk.
He walked down sidewalk after sidewalk
to see what he could discover.

He turned left and then right until he came
upon a flow of water running
across his path.

Curiously, he followed the water and eventually stumbled
into the rubber boot of a tall, strong looking gentleman.
He was washing a fire truck in front of a fire station.

"Why hello, little guy. My name is Nicholas.
What's your name?" the man asked as he looked down.

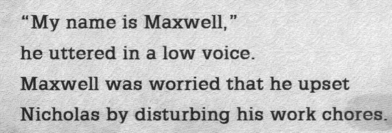

"My name is Maxwell,"
he uttered in a low voice.
Maxwell was worried that he upset
Nicholas by disturbing his work chores.

Then, Nicholas got down on his hands and knees and in a soft, gentle voice said, "I sure could use a helper around here. Are you up for the job?"

Maxwell couldn't believe it. He was only in the city one day and already had a job!

"ABSOLUTELY!" he yelled with joy. "Great!" Nicholas said, "Then a fire mouse you shall be!" Maxwell thought to himself, "I'm finally going to be somebody!"

Maxwell decided to help first by cleaning the fire truck.

He walked up to a long handled brush that was used to clean the large, shiny wheels.

" I could clean the wheels because I don't have to climb on anything," he said.

But when Maxwell grabbed the long handle, he discovered the brush was too

big to raise above his head, let alone scrub anything. His hands were too small.

Maxwell was determined to help in some way.
Next he tried to grab a wet sponge to clean the front bumper,
but the water made the sponge way too heavy.
Maxwell realized he couldn't help Nicholas with the cleaning,
and he walked away sad.

He felt like he was at the farm all over again.
"That's all right, Maxwell," Nicholas said with a smile.
"There will be other things you can help with. Everyone has a purpose."

Nicholas gave Maxwell a tour of the fire station and his new home.
Maxwell got to meet all of the firefighters that worked there.
He got to see the large, shiny brass pole that the firefighters slid down
if they were upstairs when an alarm sounded.

He also saw the areas where the firefighters slept at night.
Nicholas made Maxwell his own tiny, comfortable bed to sleep in.
He wanted Maxwell to feel at home and part of their team.
And if all of that wasn't enough, the firefighters placed ramps all over the
station so that Maxwell wouldn't have any trouble getting around.

The next day came, and Maxwell had his first alarm.
They received a call to help Mrs. Winslow
up off of the floor. She had slipped on her
carpet and needed help back onto her sofa.
Maxwell was very excited and couldn't wait to help.

When they arrived, they noticed that
Mrs. Winslow had injured her leg
and was unable to stand.

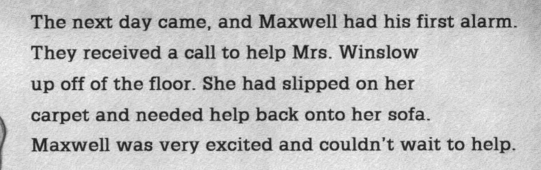

It was going to take Maxwell and
all three firefighters a great deal
of strength to lift her up.

Nicholas asked Maxwell to watch from the side so Maxwell wouldn't
risk getting stepped on. He listened to what he was told to do but was sad
because he couldn't help his firefighter friends.
"That's all right, Maxwell," Nicholas said with a smile.
"There will be other things you can help with. Everyone has a purpose."

On the next day, Maxwell and the firefighters were called to a car accident.
He thought to himself, "Now I'm going to have my chance to help someone!"
They arrived on the scene where two cars had bumped into each other.
The car doors were stuck, and the people inside the cars were unable to get out.
This job needed very heavy tools to open the doors.

Nicholas turned around to Maxwell and said,
"Please stay here and let me know
if you see anything dangerous.
The tools we are going to use are too heavy for you."
Maxwell felt like a balloon that had lost all of its air.
All he wanted was to do something useful.
He wanted to have a responsible
job and help those around him.

The firefighters rescued the people out of their cars.

Luckily, everyone was all right.

Nicholas came back to the fire truck and saw that Maxwell was sad.

"That's all right, Maxwell," Nicholas said with a smile.

"There will be other things you can help with. Everyone has a purpose."

Maxwell wasn't sure if he could believe Nicholas anymore.
Many chances had come, but he was still unable to help with anything.
He thought about going back home to the farm.
At least there, he would be with his family. He decided to go to sleep
and wait until the morning. He wanted to talk about it with Nicholas, too,
because they had become best friends in the short time since
they had met in front of the fire station.

During the night, the fire bells began to ring.
There was a large fire at a nearby school. Maxwell jumped into Nicholas's pocket
and down the brass pole they slid. They all put on their fire clothing,
jumped into the fire truck, and drove off to the fire.
The lights were flashing brightly, and the siren was blaring loudly.

Maxwell could smell smoke in the air as they approached the school.

Fire was blasting out of the second floor window.

The school custodian, Mr. Bunn,

was waiting outside.

He noticed smoke coming out of the window

when he arrived to clean the school.

"I called 911 as soon as I could!"

He exclaimed.

Nicholas and the other firefighters grabbed the fire hose
and pulled it into the doorway of the school. "You forgot about me!"
Maxwell yelled loudly from the fire truck. Nicholas thought
that Maxwell was in his fire coat pocket. He didn't know
Maxwell stepped out of his pocket to get his fire helmet on.
It was too late now.
Nicholas and the others were already up the stairs going to fight the fire.

Maxwell heard an announcement on the fire radio. It was Nicholas's voice.
"I know that is Nicholas's voice,
but he sounds different. He sounds scared," Maxwell thought.
Over the radio, Nicholas explained that he and the others were trapped.
He described the room and said that it had a statue in it.
There was a back door in the room, but they didn't have the key to get out.

Mr. Bunn was also listening with Maxwell as Nicholas was talking on the radio. "I know that room!" Mr. Bunn yelled. "And I have the key here in my pocket!"

Mr. Bunn pulled out a shiny, silver key that was attached to a small ring. Maxwell had an idea.

After asking Mr. Bunn about the quickest way to the room,
Maxwell placed the key ring around his neck
and darted into the school as quickly as he could.

Maxwell thought about how scared his friends were, and he thought
about all of the wonderful things they had done for him.
Once he was inside, he discovered there was one BIG problem.

The fire had caused a lot of damage already.
He came across fallen school desks, tables, and other things
that grown people wouldn't be able to get through,
but a tiny mouse could.

Maxwell gathered all of the courage that he had deep inside his small body. He jumped and climbed, ran and ducked through small openings that were in his way. Maxwell was NOT going to let them down.

The room next to Nicholas was hot and filled with lots of smoke.
Maxwell found a small crack under the doorway
where Nicholas and the others were trapped.

"Maxwell!" Nicholas exclaimed. "What are you doing here!?
I'm sure glad to see you!"
Maxwell pulled the key from around his neck and handed it to Nicholas.
He quickly jumped onto Nicholas's shoulder and said,
"I'm hot! Let's get out of here!"

Nicholas used the key to open the back door.
Through the door was a hallway that led outside.
Everyone made it out safely,
and the fire was put out.
"You saved our lives, little buddy,"
Nicholas said thankfully.
"Nobody could have gotten to us,
and we would have never escaped if you
wouldn't have brought us
that special key."

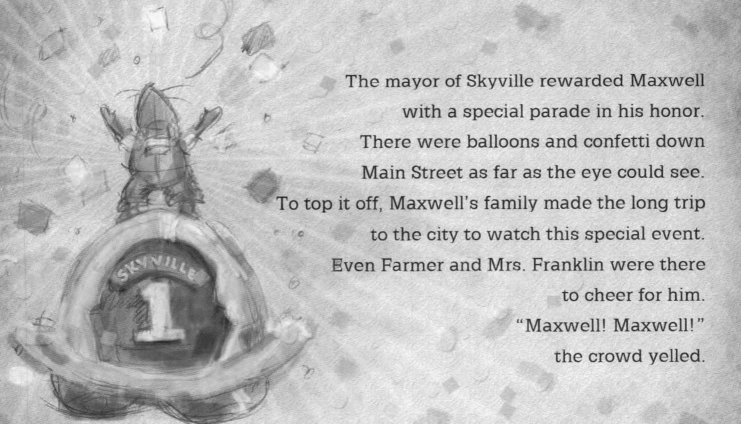

The mayor of Skyville rewarded Maxwell
with a special parade in his honor.
There were balloons and confetti down
Main Street as far as the eye could see.
To top it off, Maxwell's family made the long trip
to the city to watch this special event.
Even Farmer and Mrs. Franklin were there
to cheer for him.
"Maxwell! Maxwell!"
the crowd yelled.

After the parade, Nicholas and the other firefighters met with Maxwell
in the front of the fire station.
Nicholas reached in his pocket and pulled out a bright,
golden piece of metal.

It was a special badge that read, "Maxwell-Firehouse Mouse."

"WOW!" he exclaimed, "For me!?"

"You bet, little buddy. You definitely have earned it,

and we are so very proud of you," Nicholas explained.

Maxwell felt a warmness in his chest that he had never felt before.
He may not have been big on the outside,
but on the inside, he had a heart bigger than he,
or anyone else could have imagined.

Maxwell had found his purpose.

The End

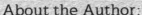

About the Author:

Michael S. Cangelosi was born and raised in Kansas City, Missouri.
He currently is a Captain with the Independence, Missouri Fire Department
along with serving as a Registered Nurse.
Witnessing many life events inspired him to write his first children's book,
Maxwell the Firehouse Mouse. When not working, you can
find him woodworking, fishing and making pizza and bread out
of his self-made pizza oven. He currently resides in Gladstone, Missouri
with his wife Grace and twin daughters, Laurena and Isabella.
You can visit him at www.ImmaginareWorksLLC.com.

About the Artist:

Sam M. Cangelosi was born and raised in Kansas City, Missouri.
A graduate of The Kansas City Art Institute - Illustration/Design Major.
Sam is a former Hallmark Card Artist and current designer at Liberty Hospital.
When not working, you can find him at the ballpark, freelancing or fly-fishing
with friends. He also currently resides in Gladstone, Missouri
with his wife Margie and sons Ryan and Casey.
You can see more of his work at www.samcankc.com.

45733396R00031